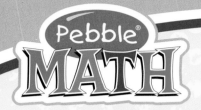

Comparing Numbers!

by M. W. Penn

Consulting Editor: Gail Saunders-Smith, PhD

CAPSTONE PRESS
a capstone imprint

Pebble Books are published by Capstone Press,
1710 Roe Crest Drive, North Mankato, MN 56003.
www.capstonepub.com

Library of Congress Cataloging-in-Publication Data
Penn, M. W. (Marianne W.), 1944–
  Comparing numbers! / by M. W. Penn.
    p. cm. — (Pebble books. Pebble math)
  Includes bibliographical references and index.
  Summary: "Simple rhyming text and color photographs describe more than, less
than, and equal to in comparing numbers"—Provided by publisher.
  ISBN 978-1-4296-7561-1 (library binding) — ISBN 978-1-4296-7874-2 (paperback)
  1. Number concept—Juvenile literature. I. Title.
  QA141.3.P45 2012
  513—dc23   2011029945

Note to Parents and Teachers

The Pebble Math set supports national mathematics standards
related to algebra and geometry. This book describes and
illustrates comparing numbers. The images support early readers
in understanding the text. The repetition of words and phrases
helps early readers learn new words. This book also introduces
early readers to subject-specific vocabulary words, which are
defined in the Glossary section. Early readers may need assistance
to read some words and to use the Table of Contents, Glossary,
Read More, Internet Sites, and Index sections of the book.

Printed in the United States of America in Stevens Point, Wisconsin.

012013   007118R

Table of Contents

How Do You Compare?

Each time you compare numbers

Just 3 choices will do!

Each number can only be

Less than <

Greater than >

Or equal to =

Greater, Less, or Equal

To compare these numbers,

Count each person's rings.

A number is less than another

When it counts fewer things.

$$2 < 4$$

Some numbers are greater than others.

They count a bigger share.

Who holds the bigger number?

Can you count and compare?

6 > 3

10

Puppies playing in the dog park;

Every child has a pup.

Match the children to their puppies.

Equal numbers will match up.

3 = 3

Let's Compare!

Count the fingers in one mitten.

Count the toes in one shoe.

Count the pennies in one nickel.

More than, less than, equal to?

$$5 = 5 = 5$$

14

A wagon has 4 round wheels.

A tricycle has only 3.

A bicycle has 2 round wheels.

Which one has the least to see?

3 turtles on the pillow.

5 cats on the bedpost.

10 monkeys on the desktop.

Can you order least to most?

$$3 < 5 < 10$$

0 is less than 100.

40 is greater than 10.

Put all these numbers in order.

Now compare again.

$$0 < 10 < 40 < 100$$

Numbers are the same or different.

You can compare and not guess!

If the numbers aren't equal (=),

One is greater (>), one is less (<).

8 > 1

Glossary

compare—to look closely at things in order to learn ways they are alike or different

equal—the same as something else in size, number, or value

greater than—more than; the open side of the sign > faces which number is greater

less than—fewer than; the pointed or smaller side of the sign < points to which number is less

Read More

Mattern, Joanne. *More Than, Less Than.* Little World Math Concepts. Vero Beach, Fla.: Rourke Pub., 2011.

Penn, M. W. *It's Addition!* Pebble Math. Mankato, Minn.: Capstone Press, 2011.

Walton, Rick. *Pig, Pigger, Piggest: Adventures in Comparing.* Salt Lake City, Utah: Gibbs Smith, 2011.

Internet Sites

FactHound offers a safe, fun way to find Internet sites related to this book. All of the sites on FactHound have been researched by our staff.

Here's all you do:

Visit *www.facthound.com*

Type in this code: 9781429675611

Super-cool stuff!

Check out projects, games and lots more at
www.capstonekids.com

Index

Word Count: 202
Grade: 1
Early-Intervention Level: 15

Editorial Credits
Gillia Olson, editor; Bobbie Nuytten, designer; Sarah Schuette, photo stylist;
    Marcy Morin, studio scheduler; Kathy McColley, production specialist

Photo Credits
All photos by Capstone Studio: Karon Dubke except: Shutterstock: Alexia Kruscheva,
10 (bottom right), Eric Isselée, 10 (top right, middle left), Gelpi, 10 (top left, bottom
left), Yuri Arcurs, 10 (middle right)

The author dedicates this book to Michael Siuta and the Ten County Mathematics
Educators Association (New York).